LABYRINTH AND THE SONG OF SONGS

LABYRINTH AND THE SONG OF SONGS

JILL KIMBERLY HARTWELL GEOFFRION

The Pilgrim Press   Cleveland

This work of my heart is dedicated with gratitude to:
God, who has expressed such love through the labyrinth,
Cheryl Felicia Dudley, who told me late one night in Chartres,
"You need to read the Song of Songs tomorrow," and
Tim Geoffrion, whose loving presence in my life prepared
the soil of understanding.

The Pilgrim Press, 700 Prospect Avenue, Cleveland, Ohio 44115-1100
pilgrimpress.com
Copyright © 2003 Jill Kimberly Hartwell Geoffrion

Image of the Chartres Cathedral Labyrinth © 2003 Robert Ferré, used by permission.

Scripture quotations are from the New Revised Standard Version of the Bible, © 1989
by the Division of Christian Education of the National Council of Churches of Christ
in the United States of America and are used by the permission.

08   07   06   05   04   03   5   4   3   2   1

Library of Congress Cataloging-in-Publication Data

Geoffrion, Jill Kimberly Hartwell, 1958–
     Labyrinth and the Song of songs / Jill Kimberly Hartwell Geoffrion.
        p.   cm.
     Includes the text of the Song of Solomon in English, New Revised Standard version.
     ISBN 0-8298-1539-2 (pbk.)
     1. Labyrinths—Religious aspects—Judaism.   2. Spiritual life—Judaism.
  I. Bible. O.T. Song of Solomon. English. New Revised Standard. 2003.   II. Title.

BM723.G46   2003
248.4'6—dc21

                                                            2003040456

Contents

Prologue

THE CHARTRES CATHEDRAL LABYRINTH

I was on pilgrimage in Chartres, France when a close friend challenged me to sit in the cathedral and read the biblical book Song of Songs. Her unexpected suggestion cut to the center of my being as holding the possibility for profound insight. I took my Scriptures to the cathedral, found a chair where one foot could rest on the limestone and marble face of the labyrinth that graces the floor, and read the entire Song in one sitting.

The explorations of physical love in the Song kept evoking memories of the love that God and I expressed during labyrinth encounters. Filled with new understanding, excitement, and incredulity I revisited the poetry, hymn texts, drawings, and prayers that had been inspired while I prayed the labyrinth. To use the language of the Song, the labyrinth had helped me know God as Lover and to be known by God as Beloved.

Geometrically Accurate Image of the Chartres Cathedral Labyrinth,
Documented by Robert Ferré

In this book I offer the biblical love story and my love story as mirrors. Both the biblical work and my text are dialogues in three voices: the Lover, Beloved, and Friends. As my words and the words of the Song of Songs rest side by side, may they lead your thinking, praying, and experiencing toward the Center.

I would like to express my deep appreciation to those who read the manuscript and offered their "care-full" comments and suggestions: Kate Christianson, Robert Ferré, Tim Geoffrion, Lea Goode, Ruth Hanna, Charlie Hartwell, John Hartwell, Lucy Hartwell, Pamela Johnson, Sally Johnson, Barbara Kellett, Kimberly Lowelle Saward, Elizabeth Nagel, and Mary Kaye Medinger.

THE SONG OF SONGS, WHICH IS SOLOMON'S.

—Song 1:1

Reflection 1 ❋ **B E L O V E D**

Let him kiss me with the kisses of his mouth!
For your love is better than wine,
    your anointing oils are fragrant,
your name is perfume poured out;
    therefore the maidens love you.
Draw me after you, let us make haste.
    The king has brought me into his chambers.

—Song 1:2–4a

RECEIVING NOURISHMENT

Drawn back
to Your breast,
my Love.

Gratefully returning
to Your roundness.

Snuggling deeply;
suckling eagerly.

Warmly and sweetly comforted
as hunger cries within.

Reflection 2 ❀ F R I E N D S

We will exult and rejoice in you;
    we will extol your love more than wine;

—*Song 1:4b*

A LABYRINTH DEDICATION

Form a loose circle with all standing on the labyrinth. Invite all to extend the energy that is in their hearts and minds through their hands toward the labyrinth.

The communal response for all who are able will be to place both hands on the labyrinth and pray, "We bless this labyrinth."

Invite each person to call forth the image of a loved one walking this labyrinth and receiving what is needed. (Pause)

Now invite all to imagine someone who it feels difficult, if not impossible, to like or accept walking this labyrinth and receiving what they need. (Pause)

One: With hearts extending in many directions, Let us pray . . .
Sacred Sustainer, Way to wholeness, Creator of possibilities, Supporter of development, Forgiving Releaser, Freedom, Honesty, Hope, Joy . . . we thank you for the beautiful spiritual tool on which we are standing. It is our intention to bless it.
Community: We bless this labyrinth.
One: May springs of openness bubble forth here; may their energies kiss the feet of all who meander on the path.
Community: We bless this labyrinth.
One: May those who come here perceive your loveliness with all of who they are—their eyes, the soles of their feet, their breath, heartbeats, muscles, minds, and sense of balance.
Community: We bless this labyrinth.
One: Thank you for welcoming the hopes that are brought here, as well as pains, questions, sighs, laughter, tears, and expressions of surprise.
Community: We bless this labyrinth.
One: Thank you for gifting us with a sacred space where we can experience your love as safety, rest, patience, kindness, goodness, hope, and healing.
Community: We bless this labyrinth.
One: Out of our gratitude we each silently offer our own prayer of blessing for this labyrinth.
(Long pause)
All: We bless this labyrinth.
One: Amen!

Reflection 3 ❀ **B E L O V E D**

rightly do they love you

—*Song 1:4c*

TRUE DEVOTION

Labyrinth,
I love you!

Old, worn, smooth stones,
I love you
as you are—
just as you are!

I love you
for how you love me,
for how you let God love me through you.

I love you
for your ability to endure through the ages.

In you
I see the stories
of my tradition
and my life.

On you
I find the ground of my being
and the dreams of my soul.

What is foreground?
What is background?
It is not important.

You bless me
coming
and going.

You ask me
to walk sincerely
promising
limitless possibilities.

Beauty
surrounds you.

Beauty
emerges from me
as I let you open me.

Such simplicity!
Such complexity!

The call inward.
The call outward.

Union,
then separation.

You remain grounded
in the shadows of incredible heights.

You provide such safety.
I accept this
and your many, many gifts
with gratitude,
awe,
and joy.

Labyrinth,
I love you!

Reflection 4   ❀   **BELOVED**

I am black and beautiful,
    O daughters of Jerusalem,
like the tents of Kedar,
    like the curtains of Solomon.
Do not gaze at me because I am dark,
    because the sun has gazed on me.
My mother's sons were angry with me;
    they made me keeper of the vineyards,
    but my own vineyard I have not kept!
Tell me, you whom my soul loves,
    where you pasture your flock,
    where you make it lie down at noon;
for why should I be like one who is veiled
    beside the flocks of your companions?

—*Song 1:5–7*

MORE THAN THE SUM OF THE PARTS

The labyrinth
is strange territory
indeed!

Physically,
it can be mapped.

But there is no telling
where I will go
once the path is entered
with a desire
to let happen
whatever
will.

Reflection 5   ❖   **F R I E N D S**

If you do not know,
    O fairest among women,
follow the tracks of the flock,
    and pasture your kids
    beside the shepherds' tents.

—*Song 1:8*

WITNESSING OTHERS ON THE LABYRINTH

We can watch,
but we cannot see
what is within—
what is emerging—
or what is being revealed.

Yet we look,
and as we gaze deeper,
we witness
what truly is.

Reflection 6 ❖ LOVER

I compare you, my love,
 to a mare among Pharaoh's chariots.
Your cheeks are comely with ornaments,
 your neck with strings of jewels.
We will make you ornaments of gold,
 studded with silver.

—Song 1:9–11

A MIRROR

I am
a mirror
in which you can gaze
at your goodness,
beauty,
joyfulness,
and loveliness.

Reflection 7 ✤ **BELOVED**

While the king was on his couch,
    my nard gave forth its fragrance.
 My beloved is to me a bag of myrrh
    that lies between my breasts.
My beloved is to me a cluster of henna blossoms
    in the vineyards of En-gedi.
Ah, you are beautiful, my love;
    ah, you are beautiful; your eyes are doves.
Ah, you are beautiful, my beloved,
    truly lovely.
Our couch is green.

—Song 1:12–16

REMEMBERING WITH ANTICIPATION

You are more than your builders' intentions
far more than limestone, marble, and mortar.
You are more powerful than the collection of prayers
which continue to be left with you.

Even as I grieved our separation,
I celebrate our coming reunion.

You beckon me,
"Come, Jill, come."

Trusting the depth of my desire,
I approach.

My love,
need,
devotion,
openness,
longings,
curiosity,
destiny,
lead me back
into your welcoming arms.

Reflection 8   **LOVER**

The beams of our house are cedar,
    our rafters are pine.

—*Song 1:17*

A PROMISE

All
that is needed
will be provided.

Trust me.

Reflection 9 ❁ BELOVED

I am a rose of Sharon,
    a lily of the valleys.

—Song 2:1

WHAT IS

My breath is my prayer.
Integration is vibrating through my cells.
I am more than I thought.
Hunger for mystical union churns within.
My life is flowing in the current of the Divine River.
Such is the beauty I embody.

Reflection 10 ❀ **L O V E R**

As a lily among brambles,
    so is my love among maidens.

—*Song 2:2*

WHY YOU HAVE COME

You are here—

touching the labyrinth
with your feet,
and cradling the labyrinth
with your heart—

to be known
and loved
by Me.

Reflection 11   ❈   **B E L O V E D**

As an apple tree among the trees of the wood,
    so is my beloved among young men.
With great delight I sat in his shadow,
    and his fruit was sweet to my taste.
He brought me to the banqueting house,
    and his intention toward me was love.
Sustain me with raisins,
    refresh me with apples;
    for I am faint with love.
O that his left hand were under my head,
    and that his right hand embraced me!
I adjure you, O daughters of Jerusalem,
    by the gazelles or the wild does:
do not stir up or awaken love
    until it is ready!

—*Song 2:3–7*

PRAYING FROM THE CENTER

God,
May I see,
truly see.

See You—
bubbling forth—
Pure,
Strong,
Robust,
Refreshing.

God,
May I see,
truly.

Reflection 12   ✿   **B E L O V E D**

The voice of my beloved!
    Look, he comes,
leaping upon the mountains,
    bounding over the hills.
My beloved is like a gazelle
    or a young stag.
Look, there he stands
    behind our wall,
 gazing in at the windows,
    looking through the lattice.
My beloved speaks and says to me:
    "Arise, my love, my fair one, and come away;
 for now the winter is past,
    the rain is over and gone.
 The flowers appear on the earth;
    the time of singing has come,
    and the voice of the turtledove is heard in our land.
The fig tree puts forth its figs,
    and the vines are in blossom;
    they give forth fragrance.
Arise, my love, my fair one, and come away.

—*Song 2:8–13*

WALKING THE LABYRINTH (A HYMN TEXT)

Sing to the tune of "For the Beauty of the Earth"
(by Folliot S. Pierpont, 1864,
music by Conrad Kocher, 1838;
DIX 77.77.77)

To your open mouth we come,
Pausing with expectancy.
Posing questions, praying dreams,
Gath'ring courage, hope, and faith,
Circle, you hold life indeed.
With thanksgiving we proceed.

Stepping in, the way is sure,
Pacing comes in its own time.
Breathing slows, awareness dawns,
Trusting, longing fill our hearts.
Pathway, you hold life indeed.
With thanksgiving we proceed.

In the center we are held,

Deeply knowing, deeply known.

Healing, wholeness rising up,

Wisdom, insight overflow.

Center, you hold life indeed.

With thanksgiving we proceed.

Back we go, the way we came,

Weaving, winding in and out.

Moving t'ward the world beyond,

Op'ning hearts to needs perceiv'd.

Pathway, you hold life indeed.

With thanksgiving we proceed.

Once outside we gaze within,

Wond'ring at the peace we know.

Spending moments filled with awe,

Taking leave with strength renewed.

Circle, you hold life indeed.

With thanksgiving we proceed.

Reflection 13 ✤ LOVER

O my dove, in the clefts of the rock,
    in the covert of the cliff,
let me see your face,
    let me hear your voice;
for your voice is sweet,
    and your face is lovely.
Catch us the foxes,
    the little foxes,
that ruin the vineyards—
    for our vineyards are in blossom."

—Song 2:14–15

I UNDERSTAND

As the floor,
gracefully I reach
across the nave.

On your way,
you walk over me
unaware.

I await you,
ready.

"Follow the path,"
my stones beckon.

Shaped, formed,
hewn ever so carefully,
my lines and curves
invite your explorations.

Walk over me if you must.
Walk on me if you can.

Reflection 14 ✸ BELOVED

My beloved is mine and I am his;
    he pastures his flock among the lilies.
Until the day breathes
    and the shadows flee,
turn, my beloved, be like a gazelle
    or a young stag on the cleft mountains.

—*Song 2:16–17*

LOOKING AT GOD THROUGH THE LABYRINTH

Beauty,
Thank You
for this possibility,
for all Your possibilities.

Truth,
Thank You
for calling to me,
for Your multitudinous callings.

Love,
Thank You
for knowing me intimately,
so very intimately.

It is so.

Reflection 15 BELOVED

Upon my bed at night
    I sought him whom my soul loves;
I sought him, but found him not;
    I called him, but he gave no answer.
"I will rise now and go about the city,
     in the streets and in the squares;
I will seek him whom my soul loves."
    I sought him, but found him not.
The sentinels found me,
    as they went about in the city.
"Have you seen him whom my soul loves?"
Scarcely had I passed them,
    when I found him whom my soul loves.
I held him, and would not let him go
    until I brought him into my mother's house,
    and into the chamber of her that conceived me.
I adjure you, O daughters of Jerusalem,
    by the gazelles or the wild does:
do not stir up or awaken love
    until it is ready!

—*Song 3:1–5*

AFTERGLOW

Beauty,
You hold me.

Body
to body.

Spirit
to spirit.

Resting
on your strength.
Secure
in your love.
Certain
of your enduring faithfulness.

My eyes
open,
my heart
expands,
and my core
twirls with joy.

Reflection 16 **BELOVED**

What is that coming up from the wilderness,
like a column of smoke,
perfumed with myrrh and frankincense,
with all the fragrant powders of the merchant?
Look, it is the litter of Solomon!
Around it are sixty mighty men
of the mighty men of Israel,
all equipped with swords
and expert in war,
each with his sword at his thigh
because of alarms by night.
King Solomon made himself a palanquin
from the wood of Lebanon.
He made its posts of silver,
its back of gold, its seat of purple;
its interior was inlaid with love.
Daughters of Jerusalem,
come out.
Look, O daughters of Zion,
at King Solomon,
at the crown with which his mother crowned him
on the day of his wedding,
on the day of the gladness of his heart.

—*Song 3:6–11*

WHAT ARE YOU?

You are just a bunch of stones!
Limestones—
quarried within four miles of Chartres cathedral.

You are a group of circles—
some huge,
others smaller,
each essentially like the others.

You are a design,
one of many sacred messengers
gathered in this place.

You are a pathway,
meandering back and forth,
forth and back,
back and forth.

You are a tool,
waiting patiently
beneath hundreds of chairs,
for whomever might come.

Ah, but you are more . . .
so much more!

Reflection 17 ✿ **LOVER**

How beautiful you are, my love,
    how very beautiful!
Your eyes are doves
    behind your veil.
Your hair is like a flock of goats,
     moving down the slopes of Gilead.
Your teeth are like a flock of shorn ewes
    that have come up from the washing,
all of which bear twins,
    and not one among them is bereaved.
Your lips are like a crimson thread,
    and your mouth is lovely.
Your cheeks are like halves of a pomegranate
    behind your veil.
Your neck is like the tower of David,
    built in courses;
on it hang a thousand bucklers,
    all of them shields of warriors.
Your two breasts are like two fawns,
    twins of a gazelle,
     that feed among the lilies.

—Song 4:1–5

BE OPEN

I invite you to pray
for eyes to see
as I see,
and
a heart to understand
as I understand.

Reflection 18   ❁   **L O V E R**

Until the day breathes
    and the shadows flee,
I will hasten to the mountain of myrrh
    and the hill of frankincense.
You are altogether beautiful, my love;
    there is no flaw in you.

—*Song 4:6–7*

DIVINE APPRECIATION

Look at the light
shining out from your eyes!

When weary travelers
rest in your presence, I rejoice.

How you create sacred ceremonies
with joy!

I am grateful that you lead
with courage.

Your silent communion with me
is so enjoyable.

It warms my heart when you acknowledge fear,
then move on.

Your beauty is most radiant
as we connect profoundly.

Reflection 19 ❊ LOVER

Come with me from Lebanon, my bride;
    come with me from Lebanon.
Depart from the peak of Amana,
    from the peak of Senir and Hermon,
from the dens of lions,
    from the mountains of leopards.

—*Song 4:8*

INVITATION TO WHAT?

After I invited you
to go on a pilgrimage
to the labyrinth in Chartres, France,
you excitedly wondered,
"Why?"

It is not important to know—
yet.

I'm glad you are coming.

Reflection 20 ❊ LOVER

You have ravished my heart, my sister, my bride,
    you have ravished my heart with a glance of your eyes,
    with one jewel of your necklace.
How sweet is your love, my sister, my bride!
    how much better is your love than wine,
    and the fragrance of your oils than any spice!
Your lips distill nectar, my bride;
    honey and milk are under your tongue;
    the scent of your garments is like the scent of Lebanon.
A garden locked is my sister, my bride,
    a garden locked, a fountain sealed.
Your channel is an orchard of pomegranates
    with all choicest fruits,
    henna with nard,
nard and saffron, calamus and cinnamon,
    with all trees of frankincense,
myrrh and aloes,
    with all chief spices—
a garden fountain, a well of living water,
    and flowing streams from Lebanon.

—*Song 4:9–15*

DESIRE

You ask, "In what ways do I want you?"

I want to know you in your body.
I want to know you in your spirit.
I want to know you in your mind.

All of you—
I want all of you:
your hesitancies,
your impatience,
your interests,
your questions,
your awe,
your misgivings,
your weaknesses,
your strengths . . .

I desire to be united with you.

Reflection 21 — **BELOVED**

Awake, O north wind,
  and come, O south wind!
Blow upon my garden
  that its fragrance may be wafted abroad.
Let my beloved come to his garden,
  and eat its choicest fruits.

—*Song 4:16*

MORNING DEVOTION

With one foot on the path,
resting,
waves of Beauty
wash over me.

Rivers of Grace
flow freely around
and through me.

Light streams to greet me,
glowing countless invitations.

Spirit within
embraces
Spirit without.

We have begun another wondrous day
together.

Reflection 22 ✤ L O V E R

I come to my garden, my sister, my bride;
    I gather my myrrh with my spice,
I eat my honeycomb with my honey,
    I drink my wine with my milk.

—*Song 5:1a*

CENTERING

To be

here

together

is enough.

Relax.

Enjoy it!

Reflection 23   ❀   **F R I E N D S**

Eat, friends, drink,
     and be drunk with love.

—Song 5:1b

PRAYER FOR THE WOMAN LIMPING THE LABYRINTH

May the Beauty in me—
God's golden spiraling light—
be Healing in her.

Reflection 24 ❋ BELOVED

I slept, but my heart was awake.
Listen! my beloved is knocking.
"Open to me, my sister, my love,
  my dove, my perfect one;
for my head is wet with dew,
  my locks with the drops of the night."
 I had put off my garment;
  how could I put it on again?
I had bathed my feet;
  how could I soil them?
My beloved thrust his hand into the opening,
  and my inmost being yearned for him.
I arose to open to my beloved,
  and my hands dripped with myrrh,
my fingers with liquid myrrh,
  upon the handles of the bolt.

—*Song 5:2–5*

CAN I WALK THE LABYRINTH TODAY?

Such pulling
and pushing within,
God.

Longing for connection,
fearful of intimacy . . .

You,
so patient—

I,
in my impatience,
barely notice.

Thank You
for waiting
while I draw up a bucket of courage
from the well of hope
where You reside
within me.

Amen.

Reflection 25 ❄ BELOVED

I opened to my beloved,
    but my beloved had turned and was gone.
My soul failed me when he spoke.
I sought him, but did not find him;
    I called him, but he gave no answer.
Making their rounds in the city
    the sentinels found me;
they beat me, they wounded me,
    they took away my mantle,
    those sentinels of the walls.
I adjure you, O daughters of Jerusalem,
    if you find my beloved,
tell him this: I am faint with love.

—Song 5:6–8

HERE I AM, BUT WHERE AM I?

I was anticipating moving out
when the path turned in.

Here I am.
But where am I?

Longing to trust
the Way,
I will walk on.

Reflection 26 ❁ F R I E N D S

What is your beloved more than another beloved,
    O fairest among women?
What is your beloved more than another beloved,
    that you thus adjure us?

—*Song 5:9*

WITNESSING LABYRINTH ENCOUNTERS IN CHARTRES CATHEDRAL

- Some stopped with quizzical looks. They saw the labyrinth, but didn't seem to be able to understand what it was or how it worked.
- Others never noticed the labyrinth on the floor as they passed over it.
- A child, about five years old, approached the labyrinth and announced to his family, "This is how you do it." He got down on all fours and began crawling from the entrance up the pathway.
- Many walked over the labyrinth on their way to Mass, knowing it was there, but paying no overt attention to it.
- One woman strode up the middle of the church, stood in the center of the labyrinth for half a minute, took off her shoes, and stood there for several more minutes before putting them back on and leaving.
- A businessman's cell phone rang. He took it out of his coat pocket, sat down on one of the chairs resting on the labyrinth and chatted for several minutes. When his call was finished, he got up and walked down the aisle between the chairs toward the altar.
- Others greeted the labyrinth knowingly, moving to the center where they stood briefly with their eyes closed.
- A baby in a large stroller gently bounced up and down over the labyrinth as her guardians pushed her.
- While his parents talked with friends, a six-year-old boy circled clockwise around the outer circumference of the labyrinth's center forty-two times!

Reflection 27 ❁ BELOVED

My beloved is all radiant and ruddy,
    distinguished among ten thousand.
His head is the finest gold;
    his locks are wavy,
    black as a raven.
His eyes are like doves
    beside springs of water,
bathed in milk,
    fitly set.
His cheeks are like beds of spices,
    yielding fragrance.
His lips are lilies,
    distilling liquid myrrh.
His arms are rounded gold,
    set with jewels.
His body is ivory work,
    encrusted with sapphires.
His legs are alabaster columns,
    set upon bases of gold.
His appearance is like Lebanon,
    choice as the cedars.
His speech is most sweet,
    and he is altogether desirable.
This is my beloved and this is my friend,
    O daughter of Jerusalem.

—*Song 5:10–16*

I KNOW THE LABYRINTH AS . . .

winding way

outline of God's love

pathway to wholeness

gracious invitation

place of revelation

metaphor of openness

opportunity

source of joy

symbol of the face of Christ

sacred space

bridge to the Divine

energetic flow

seeker's oasis

love concretized

journey to God

gentleness in movement

turning towards healing

transformational loving-kindness

mystical tool

dynamic pattern

mirror of my soul

harbinger of grace

holy ground

map of changing sameness

route of narrow wideness

space of holy play

way of forgiveness and forgiving

igniter of insights

link between the past, present, and future

giver of surprises

beckoner

pace gauger

changer of questions

call to rest

connector

symbol of the cycles of birth, death, and resurrection

wellspring of rejuvenation

trustworthy friend

sign of hope

link between outer and inner movements

facilitator of transparency

way in and a way out

and so much more . . .

Reflection 28 ✾ FRIENDS

Where has your beloved gone,
    O fairest among women?
Which way has your beloved turned,
    that we may seek him with you?

—*Song 6:1*

DIGGING THE LABYRINTH AT DEEP HAVEN

Emerge, dear Labyrinth.
Come into being, inch by inch by inch.

Find the curving line spray painted in the grass.
Poise the ice chipper two inches from its white center,
Jump on the top edge of the tool's flat head
embedding its metal faces in dirt.
Do the same thing on the other side of the line.

Push, pull; loosen the sod.
Push, pull, push, pull, push.
Extract the dirt and grass together—in one big clump.
Throw it into the nearby wheelbarrow.

Move down to an area of painted but uncut earth,
and repeat the process.
Again and again and again and again . . .

Prayers are poured
with emotion and sweat
into the trenches as they are prepared for bricks.

Emerge, dear Labyrinth.

Reflection 29   ❀   **BELOVED**

My beloved has gone down to his garden,
    to the beds of spices,
to pasture his flock in the gardens,
    and to gather lilies.
I am my beloved's and my beloved is mine;
    he pastures his flock among the lilies.

—*Song 6:2–3*

BRICK AND GRASS LABYRINTH IN THE YARD

Overwhelmed by the beauty I knew you would embody,
I committed myself to your realization.

But first, angels visited you in my dreams.
They had been walking your paths regularly!

Your orientation? All directions,
but you wanted to face northeast.

Soon paint shadowed your form;
the ground offered up soil, rocks, and roots.

Reformed elements took the shape of lines,
grass grew between them.

Now you await us all.
We approach with gratitude.

Reflection 30   ✿   **LOVER**

You are beautiful as Tirzah, my love,
    comely as Jerusalem,
    terrible as an army with banners.
Turn away your eyes from me,
    for they overwhelm me!
Your hair is like a flock of goats,
    moving down the slopes of Gilead.
Your teeth are like a flock of ewes,
    that have come up from the washing;
all of them bear twins,
    and not one among them is bereaved.
Your cheeks are like halves of a pomegranate
    behind your veil.
There are sixty queens and eighty concubines,
    and maidens without number.
My dove, my perfect one, is the only one,
    the darling of her mother,
    flawless to her that bore her.
The maidens saw her and called her happy;
    the queens and concubines also, and they praised her.

—*Song 6:4–9*

PRESENCE

Sit with me,
my beloved.

I want your mind to clear.
Perceive
the nature of your loveliness.

Reflection 31   ❈   **LOVER**

"Who is this that looks forth like the dawn,
    fair as the moon, bright as the sun,
    terrible as an army with banners?"

I went down to the nut orchard,
    to look at the blossoms of the valley,
to see whether the vines had budded,
    whether the pomegranates were in bloom.
Before I was aware, my fancy
    set me in a chariot beside my prince.

—*Song 6:10–12*

A QUESTION WORTH PONDERING

The question I give you
as you go on pilgrimage to Chartres is this:
How is the labyrinth in the church?

As you sit with the labyrinth there,
as you walk it,
as you write about it,
and draw it,
you will learn many things.

The wording of the question may change;
let its essence
guide you
to where you
and many others
are heading.

Reflection 32 ❀ FRIENDS

Return, return, O Shulammite!
    Return, return, that we may look upon you.

—Song 6:13a

RHYTHM

"I'll always remember the
clomp-clomp-clomp-clomp
of your shoes
on the stones
of the labyrinth
last night.

It kept the time for us.
It kept the time for me.
Thank you."

Reflection 33 ❖ LOVER

Why should you look upon the Shulammite,
as upon a dance before two armies?

—*Song 6:13b*

REALITY

I dwell within.

You know this Truth.

It is time to perceive it more deeply.

Reflection 34 ❀ **LOVER**

How graceful are your feet in sandals,
    O queenly maiden!
Your rounded thighs are like jewels,
    the work of a master hand.
Your navel is a rounded bowl
    that never lacks mixed wine.
Your belly is a heap of wheat,
    encircled with lilies.
Your two breasts are like two fawns,
    twins of a gazelle.
Your neck is like an ivory tower.
Your eyes are pools in Heshbon,
    by the gate of Bath-rabbim.
Your nose is like a tower of Lebanon,
    overlooking Damascus.
Your head crowns you like Carmel,
    and your flowing locks are like purple;
    a king is held captive in the tresses.

—Song 7:1–5

KNOWINGS

Your yearnings for union
are maturing beautifully
as you trust yourself
to walking them out.

Joyful remembrance
and determined hope
faithfully accompany you
on the path.

Your deep gratitude
passionately opens your heart,
making more room
for My encircling love.

Reflection 35 ✿ LOVER

How fair and pleasant you are,
    O loved one, delectable maiden!
You are stately as a palm tree,
    and your breasts are like its clusters.
I say I will climb the palm tree
    and lay hold of its branches.
Oh, may your breasts be like clusters of the vine,
    and the scent of your breath like apples,
and your kisses like the best wine
    that goes down smoothly,
    gliding over lips and teeth.

—Song 7:6–9

SACRED GEOMETRY

What number
expresses your essence?
Seven:
the joining of four and three—
humanity and divinity united.

What shape
reflects your essence?
The labyrinth's blooming center:
one circle
embraced by six.

Reflection 36   ❈   **B E L O V E D**

I am my beloved's,
    and his desire is for me.
Come, my beloved,
    let us go forth into the fields,
    and lodge in the villages;
let us go out early to the vineyards,
    and see whether the vines have budded,
whether the grape blossoms have opened
    and the pomegranates are in bloom.
There I will give you my love.

—*Song 7:10–12*

PREPARATION

The envisioning
and bringing forth
of the fifty-one-foot brick and grass Chartres-style labyrinth
in our front yard,
has been a joy!

I have learned
how to jump on ice crushers in order to remove sod,
how to extract near-boulders from the earth,
and how to lay bricks: 1,800 of them!

More importantly
I have learned
about praying something into reality,
about sensitively preparing
literal and spiritual soil
for sacred encounters.

What is ahead for us, labyrinth,
God only knows.
How wondrous!

Reflection 37 ❀ B E L O V E D

The mandrakes give forth fragrance,
    and over our doors are all choice fruits,
new as well as old,
    which I have laid up for you, O my beloved.
O that you were like a brother to me,
    who nursed at my mother's breast!
If I met you outside, I would kiss you,
    and no one would despise me.
I would lead you and bring you into the house of my mother,
    and into the chamber of the one who bore me.
I would give you spiced wine to drink,
    the juice of my pomegranates.
O that his left hand were under my head,
    and that his right hand embraced me!

—*Song 7:13–8:3*

WHAT I CALL YOU BESIDES "LABYRINTH"

An observation deck.
A symbol of sacred love.
A pathway of prayer.
A dance floor.
A communal space for individuals.
An invitation to embodied spirituality.
A classroom dedicated to turning.
A pattern of beauty.

Reflection 38 ❀ **BELOVED**

I adjure you, O daughters of Jerusalem,
    do not stir up or awaken love
    until it is ready!

— Song 8:4

WALKING THE LABYRINTH INSIDE CHARTRES CATHEDRAL

Part of me wonders,
"Shouldn't people be giving more respect to you, labyrinth?"

They just walk over you
without realizing the beauty and power
under their feet!

But another part of me jumps in,
"It seems more important
that people are coming into contact with you—
even if they aren't conscious of it.

As they walk through your pattern
which fills the aisle created by movable chairs,
they are engaging you—
and you are engaging them.
It's a start . . .

Perhaps more people are 'walking' you now
than would if you were totally uncovered."

Reflection 39 ✿ FRIENDS

Who is that coming up from the wilderness,
    leaning upon her beloved?

—*Song 8:5a*

WITNESSING CREATIVITY

"I enjoyed watching you
on the labyrinth.
Are you a dancer?"

"It was fun to see you
walk the labyrinth.
Are you an artist?"

Reflection 40 ❀ **BELOVED**

Under the apple tree I awakened you.
There your mother was in labor with you;
    there she who bore you was in labor.
Set me as a seal upon your heart,
    as a seal upon your arm;
for love is strong as death,
    passion fierce as the grave.
Its flashes are flashes of fire,
    a raging flame.
Many waters cannot quench love,
    neither can floods drown it.
If one offered for love all the wealth of his house,
    it would be utterly scorned.

—*Song 8:5b–7*

HEARTBEAT LULLABY

God,
May I rest my head
upon Your chest?

Oh, for Your love
to vibrate through my skin
and resonate in my deepest being.

As I snuggle into You,
feel my trust,
receive it as a gift.

The comfort of our togetherness
is the most precious love
I could ever know.

Reflection 41 ❖ **FRIENDS**

We have a little sister,
   and she has no breasts.
What shall we do for our sister,
   on the day when she is spoken for?
If she is a wall,
   we will build upon her a battlement of silver;
but if she is a door,
   we will enclose her with boards of cedar.

—*Song 8:8–9*

GROWING ON THE LABYRINTH

Greening Power of All
that has been,
is,
and will be,

Thank You
that we embody
Your Life-Giving,
Life-Sustaining Presence
as we know You
and are known by You
on this watering labyrinth.

May our roots extend widely and deeply.
May our trunks retain strength and flexibility.
May our leaves gift the world with what is needed.
May our seeds blow to the ends of the earth.

Reflection 42   ✺   **BELOVED**

I was a wall,
    and my breasts were like towers;
then I was in his eyes
    as one who brings peace.
Solomon had a vineyard at Baal-hamon;
    he entrusted the vineyard to keepers;
    each one was to bring for its fruit a thousand pieces of silver.
My vineyard, my very own,
    is for myself;
you, O Solomon, may have the thousand,
    and the keepers of the fruit two hundred!

—*Song 8:10–12*

A LOVER'S LETTER

Dear Chartres Labyrinth,
I feel as though we are always together,
even though we reside thousands of miles apart.

Soon my calloused, dirt-embedded feet
will connect with your pocked, worn skin.

What will we communicate
in that long-awaited embrace?

I can't imagine,
yet I'm very devotedly yours,

Jill

Reflection 43 ❀ LOVER

O you who dwell in the gardens,
my companions are listening for your voice;
let me hear it.

—*Song 8:13*

MANTRA

"Trust the process,
follow the path"
is my gift to you.

You need not panic,
or even ask (as you are!),
"Am I going the wrong way?"

Trust the process.
Follow the path.

Trust the process.
Follow the path.

Trust the process.
Follow the path.

Reflection 44   BELOVED

Make haste, my beloved,
    and be like a gazelle
or a young stag
    upon the mountains of spices!

—*Song 8:14*

"CIRCLING THE LABYRINTH" (HYMN)

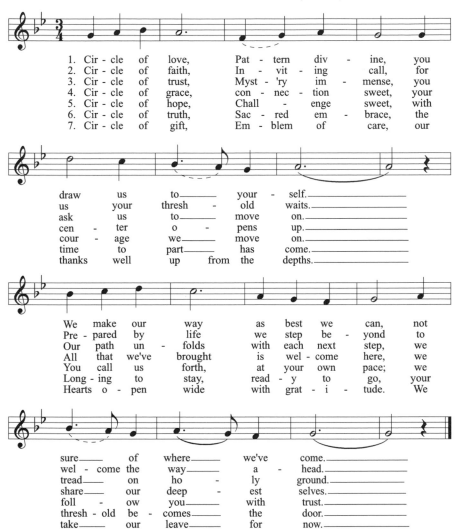

1. Cir - cle of love, Pat - tern div - ine, you draw us to_____ your - self._____ We make our way as best we can, not sure_____ of where_____ we've come._____
2. Cir - cle of faith, In - vit - ing call, for us your thresh - old waits._____ Pre - pared by life we step be - yond to wel - come the way_____ a - head._____
3. Cir - cle of trust, Myst - 'ry im - mense, you ask us to_____ move on._____ Our path un - folds with each next step, we tread_____ on ho - ly ground._____
4. Cir - cle of grace, con - nec - tion sweet, your cen - ter o - pens up._____ All that we've brought is wel - come here, we share_____ our deep - est selves._____
5. Cir - cle of hope, Chall - enge sweet, with cour - age we_____ move on._____ You call us forth, at your own pace; we foll - ow you_____ with trust._____
6. Cir - cle of truth, Sac - red em - brace, the time to part_____ has come._____ Long - ing to stay, read - y to go, your thresh - old be - comes_____ the door._____
7. Cir - cle of gift, Em - blem of care, our thanks well up from the depths._____ Hearts o - pen wide with grat - i - tude. We take_____ our leave_____ for now._____

Text: Jill Kimberly Hartwell Geoffrion, © 1999
Music: Donna B. Kasbohm, © 1999

Bibliography

Artress, Lauren. *Walking a Sacred Path: Rediscovering the Labyrinth as a Spiritual Tool.* New York: Riverhead Books, 1995.

Ayo, Nicolas, and Meinrad Craighead. *Sacred Marriage: The Wisdom of Song of Songs.* New York: Continuum International, 1999.

Barovick, Harriett. "Relaxing in the Labyrinth." *Time-Family Edition* 158, no. 8 (27 August 2001), F23.

Bolen, Jean Shinoda. "Quickening: Chartres Cathedral." In *Crossing to Avalon: A Woman's Mid-life Pilgrimage*, 22–32. San Francisco: HarperSanFrancisco, 1994.

Champion, Alex B. *Essays on Labyrinths and Other Geometric Symbols.* Philo, CA: Earth Maze Publishing, 1999.

Clift, Jean Dalby, and Wallace B. Clift. *The Archetype of Pilgrimage: Outer Action with Inner Meaning.* Mahwah, NJ: Paulist Press, 1996.

Cousineau, Phil. *The Art of Pilgrimage: The Seeker's Guide to Making Travel Sacred.* Berkeley, CA: Conari Press, 1998.

Curry, Helen. *The Way of the Labyrinth: A Powerful Meditation for Everyday Life.* New York: Penguin Compass, 2000.

Dahlke, Rudiger. *Mandalas of the World: A Meditating and Painting Guide.* New York: Sterling Publishing, 1992.

Favier, Jean. *The World of Chartres.* New York: Harry N. Abrams, 1988.

Ferré, Robert. *Constructing Labyrinths.* St. Louis, MO: One Way Press, 1996.

_____. *The Labyrinth Revival.* St. Louis, MO: One Way Press, 1996.

_____. *The Chartres Labyrinth. Trilogy.* St. Louis, MO: One Way Press, 1997.

_____. *The Origin of the Chartres Labyrinth Pattern.* St. Louis, MO: One Way Press, 1999.

_____. *Constructing the Chartres Labyrinth: An Instruction Manual.* St. Louis, MO: One Way Press, 2001.

Galland, China. *Longing for Darkness: Tara and the Black Madonna*. New York: Viking, 1990.

Geoffrion, Jill Kimberly Hartwell. *Praying the Labyrinth: A Journal for Spiritual Creativity*. Cleveland: Pilgrim Press, 1999.

———. *Living the Labyrinth: 101 Paths to a Deeper Connection with the Sacred*. Cleveland: Pilgrim Press, 2000.

Geoffrion, Jill Kimberly Hartwell, and Elizabeth Catherine Nagel. *The Labyrinth and the Enneagram. Circling into Prayer*. Cleveland: Pilgrim Press, 2001.

Kern, Hermann. *Through the Labyrinth: Designs and Meanings over 5,000 Years*. New York: Prestel, 2000.

Kidd, Sue Monk. *The Dance of the Dissident Daughter: A Woman's Journey from Christian Tradition to the Sacred Feminine*. San Francisco: Harper-SanFrancisco, 1996.

Larson, Marilyn, and Leslie Schultz. *A Pocket Guide to Labyrinths*. Northfield, MN: Chronos Unlimited, 2001.

Lonegren, Sig. *Labyrinths: Ancient Myths and Modern Uses*. Glastonbury: Gothic Image Publications, 1996.

McMillen, Joan. "Remembering the Way: Ceremony in Honor of the Labyrinth at Chartres." Menlo Park, CA: Joan Marie McMillen, 1989.

O'Roark, Mary Ann. "A Walk Through Time." *Guideposts* 54 (7 September 1999), 40–43.

Pennick, Nigel. *Mazes and Labyrinths*. London: Robert Hale, 1990.

Prache, Anne. *Chartres Cathedral: Image of the Heavenly Jerusalem*. Paris: CNRS Editions, 1993.

Sands, Helen Raphael. *The Healing Labyrinth. Finding Your Path to Inner Peace*. New York: Barrons, 2001.

Saward, Jeff. *Ancient Labyrinths of the World*. Thundersley, Essex, UK: Caerdroia, 1997.

———. *Magical Paths: Labyrinths and Mazes in the 21st Century*. London: Mitchell Beazley, 2002.

Schaper, Donna, and Carole Ann Camp. *Labyrinths from the Outside In*. Woodstock, VT: Skylight Paths Publishing, 2000.

Streep, Peggy. *The Labyrinth Garden. Spiritual Gardening: Creating Sacred Space Outdoors*. Alexandria, VA: Time Life Books, 1999 (156–63).

Villette, Jean. *The Enigma of the Labyrinth*. Translated by Robert Ferré and Ruth Hanna. St. Louis, MO: One Way Press, 1995.

Weber, Christin Lore. *Finding Stone: A Quiet Parable and Soul-Work Meditation*. San Diego: LuraMedia, 1996.

Westbury, Virginia. *Labyrinths. Ancient Paths of Wisdom and Peace*. Sydney, Australia: Lasdowne Publishing, 2001.

R e l e v a n t   W e b   S i t e s

www.gracecathedral.org: Veriditas: The World-Wide Labyrinth Project and International Labyrinth Locator

www.jillkhg.com: Jill Geoffrion's website

www.labyrinthos.net: Labyrinth resources, photo library, and archive; publisher of *Caerdroia—The Journal of Mazes and Labyrinths*

www.labyrinthsociety.org: The International Labyrinth Society

www.labyrinth-enterprises.com: Labyrinth Enterprises site with information on labyrinth construction and extensive labyrinth links

Other Books from The Pilgrim Press

LIVING THE LABYRINTH
101 Paths to a Deeper Connection with the Sacred

JILL KIMBERLY HARTWELL GEOFFRION

This book offers beginners and seasoned labyrinth users a multitude of new ways to approach this sacred tool. The short, devotional-like chapters may be used however the reader chooses—because any way that the labyrinth is approached is a right way.

0-8298-1372-1/104 pages/paper/$17.00

PRAYING THE LABYRINTH
A Journal for Spiritual Exploration

JILL KIMBERLY HARTWELL GEOFFRION

This book is a journal that leads readers into spiritual exercise of self-discovery through scripture selections, journaling questions, and poetry, with generous space for personal reflections.

0-8298-1343-8/128 pages/paper/$15.00

THE LABYRINTH AND THE ENNEAGRAM
Circling into Prayer

JILL KIMBERLY HARTWELL GEOFFRION AND ELIZABETH CATHERINE NAGEL

Gives readers an orientation in the enneagram and an explanation of the nine positions of attention that affect the ways in which we respond to the sacred and to others. Includes exercises on the labyrinth with scripture references.

0-8298-1450-7/128 pages/paper/$15.00

To order these or any other books from The Pilgrim Press call or write to:

The Pilgrim Press, 700 Prospect Avenue East, Cleveland, Ohio 44115-1100

PHONE ORDERS: 1-800-537-3394 · FAX ORDERS: 216-736-2206

Please include shipping charges of $4.00 for the first book and $0.75 for each additional book.

Or order from our web site at www.pilgrimpress.com.

Prices subject to change without notice.